# Morning Manna

## Thoughts from a Pastor's Heart

*By*

*W. Scott Creasy*

# Dedication

This work is dedicated back to Jesus, who is the author and finisher of our faith and the inspiration shared in this book.

# Acknowledgment

Many thanks to the family at Crossroads Chapel and Heaven's Saints Motorcycle Ministry, who have put their faith, trust, and support into this ministry.

# About the Author

Bishop W. Scott Creasy is an ordained Bishop and has served as senior pastor of Crossroads Chapel in Palm Harbor, Florida, for the last 29 years. He is also the International Chaplain of the Heaven's Saints Motorcycle Ministry. He has been married to his wife, Shellie, for over 35 years. They have four grown children and eight grandchildren. Scott has a heart for seeing the lost find Christ and a passion for seeing the saved go on to lead a victorious life in all the Savior has to offer.

# Table of Contents

# Fooling Yourself But You Won't Believe It

James 1:22 KJV lays out the fact that people can convince themselves that they are right with God, even when they are not.

I suppose this could be one of the worst conditions a soul could face. My reasoning for that assessment is that if an individual thinks they are on the right road, there is no need to change directions. The truth of the matter would only be revealed at the end of the road.

For the soul, the end of the road might represent a too-late scenario. Too late to forgive, too late to change, too late for love, too late for honesty, or too late to choose the truth or the right road.

Only hearing the truth can be problematic. It's the action part of the principle that engages God at His level of expectation. This is, as a follower of Christ, your reasonable service. Doing is the activator of the Word.

Unless the Word is received into the ground of a fertile heart and brings forth life, it does not fulfill its purpose. Neither does a Christian represent Christ if they fail to bring forth the fruit of the Spirit. This is exemplified in "believers" abiding in hate.

In essence, an individual can live a lie, all the while continuing religious practices. They can go to church, give in offerings, and even participate in ministries, all the while failing to love one another.

The lesson is fairly simple and truthful if you say you love God but fail to love others, you might be living a lie. If you say you are forgiven, but you fail to forgive, you may be living a lie.

Don't wait until the end of the path to ensure you're going the right way. I have some beloved friends who were on a ministry trip. They stopped for dinner. Once they were finished with their beautiful fellowship, they resumed their journey.

After traveling for an extended period, some of the road signs became confusing. It was as if their destination was further away. Well, it truly was; they had taken the wrong onramp. They traveled an hour in the wrong direction.

Although this is a little humorous, the implications spiritually are much more serious. You see after this pair realized their error, it took them another hour to get back to where they were. Spiritually, if with a lack of understanding and compassion, we offend others, we create strongholds that require even more attention.

Take a moment to check where you are heading. Is there something that you may need to repent of, someone you need to forgive, or even someone you need to show actual love to? If so, your path may not be as clear as His word.

# The Challenge

Ministry can be challenging. The highs and lows are sometimes extreme. From sharing in a family's birth of a new addition to the death of a precious loved one, the peaks and valleys can be quite the challenge.

Throughout pastoral ministry, there exists a lingering feeling of waiting for the next shoe to drop. The thoughts of what next often attempt to paint you into a corner. Betrayal, deceit, and real life all factor into everyday concerns.

What will be the next disappointment, who will be the next disappointer, seems to linger like the giant cursing your God in the valley. The voices of reality coupled with imagination seem to be an undefeatable foe.

Well, challenge accepted! I trust God. I don't trust what people think I should be or even sometimes who I think I am. However, I trust the great I Am. I trust that his will for my life will lead me through any valley, past any hardship, and position me as ultimately victorious over any giant.

I have committed my ways to the Lord to the point where I will not allow the unfaithfulness of others nor the reality of dire circumstances to impact my faithfulness. In fact, I accept the challenge. I embrace who I am in Christ and whose I am.

When the Bible tells us not to really take thought for tomorrow, even down to what we wear, I won't allow what-ifs to negatively impact my faith in Him. As a matter of fact, I'm looking to advance the cause of Christ by being what I was designed to be in Him.

It ultimately doesn't matter who does what, what storm or trial may come, or what great victory we may find. God is able to see you through the highs and lows of life and ministry. Like the old hymn says, "If we die fighting, it is no disgrace." Friends, keep on the firing line.

# Beyond The Cross

Outside of pastoring a church, I am also the International Chaplain of the Heaven's Saints Motorcycle Ministry. This ministry covers a lot of prison and street ministry. Mostly to those that are often overlooked.

As a general practice, this motorcycle ministry hands out little crosses to the people we meet during the process of daily life. We pray over those and hope beyond hope that seeds of eternity will eventually spring forth.

We often engage people who we may never see again. Sometimes weariness can have you question whether or not any progress is being made. One certain weekend provided me with the beautiful fruit of our labors.

At a yearly event where members from this ministry come together from all over, one of our brothers stopped me and shared an event that made me tear up. He was at a local Harley Shop, wearing his vest. Someone came up to him and asked if he knew me. He then shared that he had found Jesus. He specifically mentioned a little cross that had been given to him years ago.

I saw that as an answer to our prayers.

While we were away at this event, our local ministry shared with me another wonderful testimony. A friend had brought their family to church. I had met the family at one time and had given a cross to a most beautiful little girl.

The testimony was that the child had begun telling her parents about how God is Love and that He is coming back in the clouds. The child has not been to Sunday school. When asked how she knew these things, the 3-year-old responded, "God is showing me in pictures."

Our God is a miracle-working, prayer-answering, loving Father. He is drawing people of all ages. From the aged biker to the little baby, God is bringing his children home.

God, I pray that every invitation, every business card, every cross or tract would carry with it the weight of your precious Holy Spirit.

Don't be weary in well doing; we will reap if we don't give up.

# Why Stand You Here Gazing

We must have a horizontal view with a heavenly perspective. Setting your affections on things above is a scriptural admonition. However, when walking by faith, we need to have our eyes open.

I'm reminded of that moment at the ascension when the disciples received that question from above, "Why stand you here gazing." There was work to be done, souls to be won, and a great commission to fulfill.

Through faith, we look to the hills, or the Lord, for our help. Through the realization of what is at stake, we must engage the harvest. Our horizontal relationships will present opportunities for heavenly gains.

Be careful not to overlook what is lost while being found.

# Ride or Die

A friend of mine from our motorcycle ministry made a comment one night while out riding motorcycles with me. He said if you ride with me, you need to be ready to go. Lol. Now that can be taken a few different ways.

He first started off in that he was confident that since he was beside me, we would get to where we were going. Then that morphed into being right with the Lord, as I have been known to push the limits, ok sometimes exceed them. Lol.

There's some urban slang that I would like to piggyback on for this thought. It started as a "ride or die," which means someone who will be with you regardless of the situation.

Bikers are naturally a rebellious bunch. They mostly rebel against societal norms. In some forms, this brotherhood was birthed out of the brotherhood formed in actual combat. Soldiers returned from war and had a need to satisfy the loyalty that was formed in those ranks.

A good soldier would fight beside his brother until the bitter end. That same loyalty can transfer to friendship and passion. As Christians, we should be much the same.

It's appointed unto man once to die, and after that, the judgment. If you are ready to keep that appointment, life has new meaning. So, I would say die, then ride.

In essence, when we surrender our lives to Christ, death no longer holds fear. It is simply a graduation to glory. I know of many who do not ride out of fear. I have heard the words many times, dangerous, traffic, other drivers, yadda, yadda, yadda.

What we need is for some to die, then ride brothers and sisters, those who have died to Christ, and live in His glorious power. Show the world Jesus is Lord. God speed!

# Transparency

I was speaking once of God's will being done on earth as it is in heaven. My message had many references to scripture. I described the beauty of the reward that awaits the faithful.

One of the things that struck me this morning was the value of transparency. As John described the aspects of his vision, he referenced gold as pure as it could ever be,

"As transparent as glass."

If we look at the end of the story or the beginnings of an eternal chapter in Revelations, we see God's will being done in heaven. That will eventually come to earth.

As we desire to put off this earthly tabernacle, God also desires us to be clothed with the heavenly. In this vision, we see the absence of sin, we see a firm foundation, and we see that Christ is the light. All of these aspects are also aspects of the maturing Christian.

I suppose my question is, how transparent are we? We see the ultimate goal is complete transparency. With God, there is no secret thing. There is no jealousy, hatred, or darkness in Him. Scriptural references place great value on the openness and honesty required in our relationship with God.

I love the purity and freedom that are found in forgiveness. It is a beautiful thing. That type of cleansing is what can bring you complete honesty. The way of the Lord is perfect. It's designed for your benefit.

It makes me wonder if our lack of transparency leaves us rather earthy. Is your Lord visible through your flesh? Wash me, Lord, and I shall be clean. Lord, your Will be done here, now, and in us.

# The Way You Know

I have found that life is full of people who don't know where they are going. Countless souls we encounter every day have no idea of their final destination. The most concerning part of this truth is that those folks all have opinions.

Imagine taking directions from someone who doesn't know where they are or where they are going. None of us would knowingly heed those wayward directions. The thing about it is we don't stop to assess whether or not the individuals from whom we are taking directions in life actually know the truth or the way.

It starts early; some call it a sheltered life. By this, I mean that as parents, we attempt to keep our children within the bounds of what we deem as acceptable. However, the opinions of neighbors and classmates soon began to lend unwanted directions.

As a child, I did not realize that I was taking directions from someone who was lost. The end result is being lost but thinking you know where you are and where you are going. Thank God for a Way Maker. He does not leave us lost.

As Christians, we experience much of the same. We try our best to cultivate the right relationship with Christ and be a good example. Then along comes opinions I'll call winds of doctrine. Children of Christ can be influenced by wrong directions.

It all goes back to trust and truth. As children, we trust our mother and father to a degree. That degree equates to who you are and who you will be. Of course, I'm speaking of a good mother and father and also of good Christian leaders.

Trust in Christ, trust in Godly examples, trust in truth. Jesus said that in knowing Him, you will know the Way. You will also begin to hear Him through those who know Him as the way. There are many other voices, both physical and spiritual, who do not really know the way.

Be careful from whom you take directions. Be careful who you allow to speak into your life. Just like those neighbors and classmates, directions and instructions will have an impact.

# The Value of Trust

How many people in life can you really trust? I can remember a story about Young Goodman Brown, where bit by bit, everyone the character thought he could trust, eventually eroded away into the shadows of doubt.

Life has a way of exposing falsehood. Time is most usually the darkroom where these negatives are developed. You eventually learn who you can trust.

The wounds of betrayal are heartbreaking. When someone lets you down that you thought you could trust, it's devastating. Once you feel it, you never want to feel it again.

We then take steps to avoid the repeat of such emotions by a variety of tactics. Withdrawal, closings up, and setting up defenses all attempt to limit the damage. Such methods may seem beneficial emotionally. However, there may be a higher cost.

I have to admit that the longer I live, the fewer people I trust, and on the other hand, the more I value trustworthiness. Christlikeness includes being someone who can be trusted.

You know, the seeketh not their own, the friend closer than a brother, and the virtuous value can be you. The value of trust can be found in you.

All of us, at one time or another, have been less than trustworthy. Thank God, the teachings of Christ include second chances. I'm reminded of Jesus' closest friend Peter who would break a trust but then be renewed to proper order.

Knowing the pain caused by broken trust, let us strive to live out faithfulness not only to God but to one another. Show this world the value of trust.

# Context

One of the most pivotal words in Christianity is context. Basically, this references verses of scripture and how they actually apply. Time frames, subject matter, agreement, and translation; they all flow into understanding the Bible in context.

Lately, I have watched as unbelievers attack the faith by what they say the "Bible" teaches. I have also witnessed believers embracing what they think are truths to their own diminishment. One of the ugliest parts of life is what happens when one is sure of something that is not so.

One of the keys to success regarding scripture is context. Though people might still disagree about the end result, applying proper placement using the above-mentioned attributes helps us to understand hard things.

Time frames address the different systems and situations throughout Biblical history. For example, one might say the Bible teaches animal sacrifice. Well, it did, but it doesn't anymore. The sacrificial system under the Law and Moses was a passing time frame.

Without context, people can take a past truth and attempt to paint a spiritual presence that is inaccurate. The sacrificial system is only one example. Others might include the time Jesus walked the earth versus the time following His ascension. Or, then again, a time following his ascension but before the day of Pentecost. All offer perspectives in times that must be considered.

I've heard, "Well, the Bible teaches slavery or the subservience of women." In a way, both might be somewhat true, but context helps us to focus more accurately. In the days of the first century, both were actuality. That doesn't mean that the Bible promotes the practice.

The Bible itself says that in the mouth of two or three witnesses, a matter is established. How many countless disagreements could be avoided if we had the whole truth? In essence, one scripture can't be true at the expense of another. This premise screams context.

Lastly, but in no way least of all, is translation pitched against original intent. With the plethora of differing translations, it would be foolish to think that everyone persevered in God's intentions. I believe we will be overwhelmed by the misunderstanding of scripture when we see the end result.

What a work the Holy Spirit has undertaken...to lead us and guide us into all truth. May you be led today by the Holy Spirit into perfect Biblical context.

# The Middle of the Road

Of course, staying in your lane will most likely get you to your destination in the safest manner; however, when it comes to life, the middle of the road might be the best bet. I can remember a friend saying that he was entitled to his portion of the road, and he was taking his in the middle.

When it comes to a relationship with Christ, we see a broad spectrum of what people have covered under the umbrella of Christianity. I have watched as the movement as a whole might swing from one extreme to the next. It's much like a pendulum. There are extremes on both sides.

Some of the best advice that I was given as a young minister was from my paternal grandfather. He said, "Son, there will be people on the left and people on the right; get in the middle of the road and keep your eyes on Jesus." I'm not sure truer words have ever been spoken.

There are multiple facets of that statement. One that is glaring to me is to plow your own row. It's not wise to compare yourself to others when we are all measured by the stature of Christ. I have witnessed the leftist extremism of Christianity as well as the uber-religious fanaticism that tempt from both sides.

The problem for me is that if you run off the road on either side, you are still in the ditch. Whether it's the unhealthy embracing of a sinful nature or the conservative, judgmental spirit, both err from the image of Christ.

The focus must be on the example that Christ has set for us. That is the mark. That is the highest calling. I understand that to some, my projected image may fall on one side or the other, but I'm doing my best to keep it in the middle of the road.

Many may fall on either side, but the road that leads to life is doable. Keep your eyes on Jesus, and focus on that goal of being like Him and being with Him. Hit that mark.

# Saturday Morning

The morning of this writing is a Saturday, the day after what we call Good Friday. I am touched by the many public proclamations about Christ's crucifixion. However, this morning I couldn't help but think about the day after.

The disciples who walked with Jesus, who were taught by him, who were eyewitnesses, were dispersed. The shepherd had been smitten, and the sheep were scattered. Fear and uncertainty seemed to, by all accounts, have won.

I can only imagine the conflicting thoughts that must have been present. He's gone. I thought he was the one, the answer, the Savior. *What am I going to do now? Am I next? Where can I go to escape?* I watched him die.

In the middle of the greatest victory humanity has ever seen, faith was being sifted. Imaginations seemed to rule the day. Fear was the lying tongue that whispered in each ear. The future was believed lost. Hearts were broken.

Death had passed this way before. God's people had planned and practiced religiously. Surely the stories of the first Passover resonated in their hearts and minds. They were locked behind closed doors with all they held dear.

The blood was to be on the doorpost. The sacrificial lamb was slain. Inside, all there was to do was wait. Without were anguish and uncertainties. I can almost hear the physical manifestations of a spiritual reality. The death angel was coming through.

The Exodus of God's people patterned God's eternal plan. Now, all of the elements were no longer types and shadows. It was the

Lamb of God that would take away the sin of the world. That's, now, your world.

Let faith arise, and God's enemies will be scattered. When it comes to the day after and the battlefield, which is your mind, it is faith in God's plan that wins. The disciples would eventually believe once they saw the risen Savior. We can today be more blessed because we believe.

There are many parallels that I find with the circumstances that we face today. Unless you are over 100 years old, you haven't seen anything like today. Again, we find ourselves behind closed doors, imagining a myriad of outcomes. Let me assure you, we win!

This is the faith that overcomes the world. Believe with me that God knows and cares. Beyond your fears, he cares. Regardless of what is passing by outside, he cares. His blood was shed for you. That is as certain as anything you will ever hear.

The last of Christ's enemies is your death. Have you prepared for your passing over? The blood of Christ has made way for your exodus. Through faith, place your foot firmly on the head of sin and death.

Trust Jesus today for today and all of your tomorrows.

# Hands off Ministry

Covid scares have placed us into a whole new world, and we try to navigate those with wisdom, so I'll try to make this short and to the point.

Since the onset of my years of ministry, I have had a hands-on approach. Without fail, every Sunday, I have encouraged my church to greet your neighbors. Hug somebody's neck, shake someone's hand and let them know you love them is my mantra.

The conundrum of the situation flies in the face of everything we believe and practice. Don't touch, don't gather, isolate yourselves; all are exactly the opposite of normal ministry. These new waters will be a challenge. Some of us will fall. Some of us will flourish.

One thing is for certain; whatever you do, someone will disagree with it. If you cancel the service, they will disagree, and if you fail to cancel, they will disagree. I knew that the Bible said that family would turn in other family members; I just didn't think it would be over toilet paper.

I do believe drastic times call for desperate measures. Of course, there's no harm in a couple of no hugs and fist bumps instead, Sundays; however, there's a difference between temporary precautions and permanent fear. I think that's where most of us are right now.

We believe in prayer, even prayer without touching. That being said, there's also a need for the laying on of hands; it's biblical. Jesus touched the lepers. Let that settle in your spirit.

I saw someone say to check on your elderly neighbor...well, call them, maybe. You can't visit the nursing home or intensive care so pray for them from wherever you are. Do that with this truth in mind; this too shall pass. Certainly, none of us want to be a carrier or transmitter of any kind of mutant superbug, so caution is warranted.

I do find it strange that the news is telling us how to sanitize our trip to the gym, but we should limit our worship. Hmmm.

Find a way during this timeout from normal hands-on ministry to bless others. I have watched as some creative ministry opportunities have been highlighted. Be an encourager.

# What If

Urgent: What if? If you are easily offended, proceed no further.

Backdrop: It's 2020, and people are going absolutely outhouse rat crazy over the Coronavirus. I know many who have lost tens of thousands of dollars in the market. That is unless you were heavily invested in Lysol or dust masks.

It's like someone hollered snow up north or a hurricane along the coast. Suddenly, Walmart has no more wipes. Wipes are the bread, milk, and water of this new phase of life.

Just like that, one-half of the population, the half that wasn't killed by guns, are experts on communicable diseases. Forget that the sale of Corona beer is down over 40%. Um hmm. Why, we are not even supposed to pop the bubble wrap! What thieves of joy we suffer.

I'm amazed at the seemingly limitless methods of avoiding this plague. Now here's the hook. What if we avoided sin the way we avoided the possibility of getting sick?

You get it. What if the very thing that can actually cause the death of your soul were given half as much apprehension as this virus? Let's call it sinsimplex666.

What if you could catch it in the wrong crowd? Would you be more careful who you ran with? What if you could read of ways to avoid being infected? Oh, that there would be a run on the Christian Book Store for Bibles. Wouldn't it be wonderful if the Bible apps crashed for the frenzied hunger?

What if you were as quick to warn others of the impending dangers and the devastating effects of sin? What if we had a filter we could place over our mouths so we would not adversely impact others? What if we were as quick to spread the good news as we are the bad? What if you could recognize a carrier to steer clear of?

While you are thinking of the germs that might be waiting on the next shopping cart handle or the next coworker's cough, take a moment to realize there's already a death sentence. Be careful not to catch it. Be quick to offer the cure.

Fear not what sickness might rack your body; rather, be concerned about eternity and your spiritual future.

And now, back to your regularly scheduled programming.

# That's True But...

Do you realize the ones who thought they knew the written word best are the individuals who had Christ crucified? That's correct; they were so right that they put the son of God to death. How wrong could one be? I find there is not much of a difference today. The church world judges improperly, and the world claims sound judgment. It is like the truth hanging in the middle of two thieves.

Of course, I am not talking about the true church. There are those who rightly divide the Word. There are also those in the world who recognize the innocence of Jesus. It is the culmination of the dead letter versus the Spirit who gives life. A letter, the Bible, absent of the Spirit, will still produce the same death today.

I think of those who know the truth but cannot find the wind of the Spirit to live it. I think of those who imagine themselves to be spiritually wise through Biblical knowledge yet lack the very love of God that will result in life. The scripture truly is a double-edged sword. I keep thinking that is true but...not without further clarification, revelation, and explanation.

Which is more dangerous, a church that embraces blatant sin or a world that embraces a powerless church? It is the Word that says of itself that, without the Spirit, it is ineffective. It is the same Word that places boundaries on the Spirit for perfect order. For the delicate answers regarding these equations, we must look to Jesus, the author, and finisher of our faith.

To flow with the nature of Christ is our design. Anything short of that is lacking. I love the way that Jesus navigated the various obstacles that life presented. Whether it was answering a question with a better question or answering a scripture with another scripture in the perfect context, he sets the example. He calls us to Himself. Granted, it is a high calling. However, He is also able to bring us into this glory.

Not by might, nor by power but by my Spirit, says the Lord. He who began His work through the cross will be faithful to complete it by His Spirit. The "it is finished" of the cross authored our salvation. The "He is risen" of the empty tomb provides, through the Spirit, the finishing.

We must not only know the Word (it), we must know the Word (Him).

# Voices

Saying I hear voices might draw you some unwanted negative attention. However, I will guarantee that all of us do, hear voices, that is. The trick is in which one you listen to.

My thoughts come from a statement associated with an individual, who, when you think about what was said, you can hear it in the person's voice. Those with distinct voices are often mimicked because you know what they sound like.

John Wayne had a particular draw. Sam Elliott is used for every other meme on the internet because of his unique presentation. You don't have to try really hard to hear those familiar voices.

I still recall the voice of my grandfather. Certain things he would say or sing still resonate in the resources of my mind. "BOY," "That's alright, mama," and a few other phrases come to me in his voice.

I know the voice of my father, my wife, and my children. If I hear my mother, she might say, "Be sure your sins will find you out." Those are the voices I will never forget. I hear them when I think of my loved ones.

It's the strangest thing when one hears themselves recorded. The reason is we are accustomed to hearing our voice from within. Your voice is the voice that reasons through life's many choices.

Spiritually speaking, there are voices as well. What does the voice of reason sound like? Sometimes we are forced to choose between varying opinions. Many recognize the voice of both good choices and of bad. Most likely, it's the same voice, yours.

We make almost every move from an inaudible prompt. I can remember telling myself that I had to get up and go to school, and then to work, and then to face every day. Now, some people may need more prompting than others. Some may even speak to themselves for reinforcement of things that they know they need to do.

When you hear the word of God in your head/heart, whose voice is it? When you feel an unction from His Spirit, who does that sound like? Most likely, if you are like me, you can't put your finger on it, but you know it when you hear it.

I love the account in scripture of Samuel's calling. The voice was like that of his surrogate father. It was only with further fatherly advice did Samuel learn to hear the Word of God.

Friends, I desire you to hear the Word of the Lord. God is not silent. No man's opinion stops your Father from speaking. There is no speech or language where His voice is not heard. Are you hearing? He that hath an ear let Him hear.

The need for spiritual discernment has never been greater. Many say what God has said, but God hasn't said it. Many say God does not say it, but He has and does. My desire is for you to hear the most important voice in life. That is the voice that calls you to a right relationship with Christ, to deeper understanding and greater revelation. Come.

# Meectomy

Just before I began to speak at a ministry event, a couple of our brothers were discussing a book entitled "The End of Me." As I had entitled my message "The End of You," they were pleasantly surprised by the Spirit with such great confirmation.

I didn't realize that there was such a book. However, the truth of the premise unlocks for us a host of thought-provoking challenges. I will attempt to provide a synopsis of that thought process.

The scripture that sparked my inspiration comes from Jude. Just towards the end, it says, "Some save with compassion, others with fear pulling them out of the fire.' This particular verse of the Bible explains a couple of different aspects in such a simple way.

First, the need for salvation and intervention is of the utmost importance. Secondly, there are multiple ways of accomplishing the same goal. The lost need people who go the extra mile and who go to the extreme to share the light of the gospel.

Both of these approaches require self-sacrifice. Hence, the end of the individual who has submitted themselves to the process of the harvest. We must come to the end of our fleshly ability and understanding. The Bible calls it our reasonable service.

The difference between saying and doing is where this proverbial rubber meets the road. Many will say I am His, and He is mine. However, in action and lifestyle, it is the farthest thing from reality. The new testament principle is found in the text "I die daily." Of course, we know that to be dying to self is so that Christ's purposes would be revealed in our actions.

Paul stated he was crucified with Christ but continued to live with Christ as his impetus for living. For us, we could use better nails. Someone said the problem with a living sacrifice is that they wiggle. We say we are crucified with Christ. Nevertheless, we continue to live not with Christ as our motivation but with our own self in control.

The end of you is where true Christianity begins. Our actions and reactions reveal whether or not both our cross and the cross of Christ is in proper order in our lives.

At the end of your ability, you will find faith in God. Things that you could never accomplish in and of yourself now become possible. God does not worry about your tomorrow. Neither should you. At the end of your fear and anxiety, you will find that God has got this, that God has got you.

At the end of you, you will find others. Let's be honest, self-love, self-esteem, and selfies have replaced self-sacrifice. In essence, we have replaced the Holy Spirit with a lower opinion of ourselves. This world and your self will combine if allowed to form an eminence front.

It appears that you have all your ducks in a row. It appears that you have your emotions in check, but when life brings the rain, your self stands on the sand. God asks questions of us like, "Who told you that?" Or why has your countenance fallen? The truth is that our face shows our hearts' condition, and our actions tell on us.

Our own words reveal whether we are conquerors or conquered. At the end of yourself, you will find the empowerment that the world promises but can not deliver. Through submission

31

to our service to the Lord, we find the power that overcomes self and this world's trappings.

At the end of yourself, you will find the end of the agenda. It's not about you anymore. It's about the mission to seek and save that which is lost. At the end of your life, you will find that that was the most important thing.

At the end of you, you will find others and unity. People of the same mindset are unified in purpose. More of him and less of me will bring us all to the feet of Jesus. From there, we go and tell. We teach and preach; we sacrifice and move in Him. Surround yourself with those others.

At the end of you, you will find new life, new purpose, and new energy. The compelling call of Christ empowers us through His Spirit to testify and bare witness to the truth. The truth is Jesus saves. He saves us from ourselves. He saves us from the peril of hell and eternal separation from God.

He will cause us to love the unlovable. He will cause us to reach into the fire that this world kindles in an effort to save the lost.

My prayer is that we would lay down our opinions, our pride, our lusts, and in actuality, our lives so that we would reveal what it means to be children of God.

# Unmasked

I am a professional people reader. In some ways, I feel gifted with the ability. Being able to see beyond an individual's exterior is something we all do in one way or another.

However, I have noticed, of late, a bit of a problem. Part of my profession has been hampered by masks. I noticed it the other day when talking to a coworker who was wearing a surgical mask.

I could hear him speak, a bit muffled, but I could still hear. The problem was that half of his face was covered. I felt a bit hamstrung. I struggled to interpret his emotions as he spoke. It felt much like a text or email, partially void of expressions.

The thoughts of that lack helped me to realize that we deal with that on a regular basis. Though many refuse to wear surgical masks, they still mask their true self. I suppose many of us do that from time to time.

In a subtle way, we don't want to wear our feelings on our sleeves. In another, we don't want others to know our inward struggles. It reminded me of how we look on our outward appearance, but God sees the real you.

As a pastor, I know that I have masked my feelings before. I had attempted to appear strong when on the inside, I was weak. I had attempted to look whole when I was broken. The more I mature in Christ, the less I have to hide the real me.

The more we grow, spiritually speaking, the less we will feel the need to hide ourselves. If we love and forgive, as Christ forgave, it promotes undeniable honesty. It is that type of clarity and acceptance that people need to be made whole.

Two are better than one, except when it comes to faces. There are those who will continue to wear masks when our health crisis is over. Sometimes we, as believers, are the best at it.

I would like to encourage you to drop the facade. If someone asks you if you are okay, it's okay to say no. How will things get better if there's a constant denial that anything is wrong?

# Saul's Systematic Theology

If your joy is derived from letting others know why what they believe is wrong, you may want to try the spirit. Of course, that thought would be hamstrung by your limited understanding of the Spirit. Saul's theology shows this principle all too well.

According to the Law, which was the Word at that time, Saul's assault on Christianity was justified. He described himself as blameless and in total alignment with the Law. He set out to destroy those led by the actual Holy Spirit. This sounds all too familiar. It is a familiar spirit.

That critical spirit vaults itself, into position, through a religious pride of self-importance. It poses and positions itself between a God that speaks and ears that need to hear. It mimics the old evil verse echoing doubt about what God has said.

God has spoken to His people for thousands of years. Who is the man that stops God from speaking? What scripture tells of a God that stops speaking? Where can you go that His voice is not heard?

All of creation is charged by the synchronicity of His voice. From the highest height to the depth of the sea, His voice resonates. The trees obey, the sun and stars, and every creature is because He speaks. That includes you.

The Bible declares a God that speaks. This includes the beginning through to the end of this world as we know it. The voice of the tender Shepherd calls. The voice of the Holy Spirit draws. Saul's theology missed that aspect.

It took an actual experience for Saul to realize he had heard the voice, yet he had failed to respond. He had the written text. He had the authority in the flesh, but what he did not have was that ear tuned to what the Spirit would say.

Saul would meet the Word in the Spirit. His life would never be the same. The leading of the Spirit would become the most important aspect of Saul's life. Where he would go and what he would say would no longer be a simple text-based intuition.

There was no staying with the ship in scripture; he heard that from the Spirit. Saul's fear-based crusade would become Paul's missionary journey; Paul's Spirit led the missionary journey. There was no man of Macedonia in the text, but there was a divine direction in the Spirit.

The text itself describes itself as dead being alone. Saul's persecution of Christ came from his dead letter understanding. There are many dead-letter dealers operating today. There are still people killing Christians with false doctrine.

The best part of this truth is that God's voice was louder than Saul's limited comprehension of biblical doctrine. His voice will not be silenced.

If someone tells you God no longer speaks, just smile and let them go on. If they can ignore what God is saying, they won't hear you either. It's a spirit.

Saul hid behind biblical text until the light came on. There was a voice. There still is a voice. Speak, Lord, thy servants hear.

# Authority, Anointing, and Annoying

Touch not the Lord's anointed was a biblical statement used around the time of King Saul and David. In hindsight, it appears that David respected Saul as his leader even after his anointing for the office had started to wane.

David's treatment by Saul could be described as vile. One could argue that David would have been justified in taking Saul's life. He was even provided the avenue to act in such a manner multiple times. However, David seemed to have a different set of marching orders.

David's actions model us a deeper level of respect. That example gives God the ultimate say regardless of our feelings. I'm sure it was tempting for David to act. He had been anointed to be king. He had been treated poorly. It makes me wonder how we would perform in similar circumstances.

The anointing is a beautiful thing. When someone operates in their God-given talents, there is a certain satisfaction for everyone concerned. Godly authority is attractive. We see this in the life of Christ as the masses gather to hear Him speak.

When people attempt to use their authority in a less-than-anointed way, it's annoying. You have probably experienced a bad boss. It's hard to stand by and watch such a train wreck. However, in the workplace, it's amazing what we learn to endure to stay employed.

God has a way of bringing seasons to an end so that the next may begin. The first cool day of early fall tells us that another summer is passing. However, there may be a few hot days left before we experience the true break in the weather.

The Lord also oversees spiritual seasons. He teaches us to endure those less-than-pleasurable things like a good soldier. There's not a nation that rises or falls without His knowing. There's no church, pastor, president, or politician whose days are not numbered in one way or another.

Keeping faith can carry us past those annoying times. There is an anointed future. Trust God in every season. Be careful not to get ahead of His timing.

# Unchained, Unchanged, and Unchecked

In the late 70s and 80s, there was a fad of wearing a thick gold necklace with your shirt unbuttoned at the top. The look was one that seemed to be birthed out of the disco era. Silk shirts, bell bottoms, and polyester suits were normal. I am glad that that bend has mostly passed. There may be a few holding onto what was once thought to be a good look.

Sin should never be in style. When you have tasted the freedom offered in Christ, we must earnestly contend for the faith that brought us out of that bondage. Hopefully, never to be entangled in it again. Sin has a look. Whether it is in the lust-filled eyes or the pride of life, sin is visible. Well, it is to those who have known freedom in Christ. He is a chain breaker.

With that being said, the faith is filled with people of all walks and diverse levels of maturity. We often see individuals, believers, who still wear the mark of sin. Though they believe in Jesus, there has been no remission of the issues of life that keep them bound. Sin is a reproach to every people, nation, and individual. Left unchecked, sins result is deadly.

One of the approaches to sin in the modern faith is that all sin is the same, that we all sin every day, and that there is no remedy for that. You may have heard the phrase, "Don't judge me just because I sin differently than you." What does that say about the life-changing, chain-breaking gospel through the blood of Jesus Christ?

God does not teach us to continue in willful sin, simply waiting for the future day of change. As a matter of fact, He teaches us to first clean up and then help others to be clean. Which one of us would say to a brother or sister, "Hey, that rash looks good on you"? We would not, especially if we had the cure for whatever malady that had infected them.

With that in mind, why do we allow sin to ravage and go unchecked? We are taught that if we see something, we should say something. If sin is unchecked, people remain unchanged. Is there one of us who would not fight against forces that would enslave another physically? Why would you allow your brothers and sisters to die the slow spiritual death of sin?

I would rather that someone check me, that I might be unchained rather than remain unchanged.

# This Must Be What Jesus Felt Like

Sometimes in life, I have a passing feeling of familiarity that I can't quite put my finger on. The strange part is that it isn't a single emotion, and neither is it attached to an individual circumstance. However, knowing the scripture and the accounts of Christ's life, I can often identify a marker that causes me to pause and think, this must have been what Jesus felt like when...

The strange part is that it's not a one-dimensional aspect. The feelings hit in moments of both extreme joy and sorrow. His experience is realized in real life. Knowing the scripture and Christ, the feeling is remarkable.

I feel for those who suffer alone. Those that don't know Him in the way He desires to be known. I also often think about those who have none close enough to celebrate great victories. Christ has a designed relationship to fulfill the void created by being alone.

Not only does a relationship with Christ provide the comfort and friendship needed in such times, but it also creates an availability of a family of believers. Both are designed to combat those feelings of separation and isolation that plague humanity.

In life, the emotions that accompany betrayal can be paralyzing. Unless the knowledge of Christ rises up and says, I too felt that exact same way, we might be hampered. Christ endured the greatest of betrayals yet for a planned effect.

He was a man acquainted with sorrow and impacted by grief. When I feel those emotions, I gain strength through faith that my Lord knows what that feels like and has overcome.

Within the same avenue of thought are those moments of great success. Those events like when a loved one comes to faith believes, or experiences victory in Jesus. Mountain top jubilation makes us feel what Jesus felt, as well.

I think back to the reinforcing voice from heaven of the Father's pleasure. The triumphant acclaim of a realized savior certainly met the intents of God's own heart and brought to Christ that joy unspeakable and full of glory.

There's an old song by Peter Frampton that says, "Do you feel like I do." Many people never know or realize there's a friend who is closer than one might know, one who has felt just like they do.

Know this, whatever you may be going through, one has walked before and knows exactly how you feel. If you know Him, you know how we feel. If you don't, he is waiting; we are waiting, waiting for you.

# A Christian Like You Or Me

Well, Sunday's message surmised.

A Christian like you or me.

What if everyone in the church was just like you or me?

What would the church look like?

Would that be a good thing or a bad thing?

I have noticed some of the greatest critics of the Church do not attend church, they blame it on others, but the problem is inside of them. They would say the church is full of hypocrites, and they have some credibility.

That begs my point this morning.

Their criticisms would run the gamut.

Many critiques are valid; however, many are birthed in the devil's labor and delivery room to keep people from the truth, from fellowship, and ultimately from Christ.

I began to think, what if the church was full of people like me? Our women's ministry would certainly be lacking. Lol

First, let me say that God has a way of blending our diversities together to make the whole, and where one-part lacks, another fills the gap.

My message today is not so much to highlight our failures but rather to provoke one another to good works and, by so doing, a rejection of those things that might hamper our Christian witness as individuals and as the church.

*Let us provoke one another to good works.*

**Hebrews 10:24**

Provoke normally, in my mind, means to poke at and make mad, but in this sense, although it holds those aspects, it's more meant to encourage and help others realize what is at stake.

This scripture is nestled in between holding onto your faith and the fault of embracing willful sin.

What if everyone was only as faithful as you? One of the driving factors for me in becoming a Christian was the fact that I had others depending on me to lead them in the way of Christ.

The conviction of not living Christlike weighed on me as an unfulfilled destiny. It was not until my embracing of Christ's calling that the pieces of my life began to take shape.

Before long, we, as a family, were in church on a regular basis. In fact, when the doors were open, we were there. It was not long until we were the ones opening the doors.

What would the church look like if everyone attended church as you did? What if the only time that the church was open was because you had opened it? What if the church was closed when you were not there?

As Christians, our lives lead. The pattern must point to faithfulness through Christ. I struggled because I know of a scripture that says not to compare ourselves to ourselves, but I also know that Paul said follow me as I follow Christ.

Once again, I celebrate the diversity that is the body of Christ, but our individual parts need to be strengthened. What if everyone was a soul winner like you? What if everyone's conversations were modeled after yours?

Would there be a lot less talking or a lot more gossip? What if everyone encouraged others like you do? We have an opportunity to build up or tear down.

What if everyone forgave like you forgive? Would we all be forgiven, or would we all still be at fault?

What if everyone worried like you worry? Where, then, would our faith be?

The message today goes for any fault or success. If they were projected onto one another, what would the church look like?

The rub is that our individual faults through Christ would be diminished and our strengths amplified...that we would desire the best and reject the worst.

This premise must be applied to every aspect of our Christian walk, that we would walk worthy in a manner, in a model, that would show Christ in us as the hope of glory.

# What To Do With A Broken HEART

What to do with a broken heart

Should I hide my broken heart away, should I do so that no one will say

I know how you feel, or it will soon be better

Or maybe send a text or even write me a letter

Should I shout from the rooftop oh, it hurts so

Or go to a place where no one else goes

To think it all over and have a good cry

Or hold back the tears and dry my eyes

Should I be strong and encourage myself

Or withdraw inside my feelings to the shelf

Those are the questions that so many have asked, the answers elude as day by days pass

From somewhere within, that gentle voice calls

I'm mending and fixing your broken heart's walls

Can a broken heart truly live again

If given to Jesus, it's not if but when

He is near to that heart, from what I've been told

Through faith, the heart heals by heaven's own gold, what shall I do with the heart such as this,

Jesus knows what is needed, it's a heart just like His.

# Killing Christians

Many years ago, the New Testament Church sprang to life, surging with power from the Holy Ghost. It called out both sin and religion. It focused on the relationship. Infused and endowed with power from on high, the church multiplied in numbers in dramatic fashion.

Persecution was fierce. The enemy feared what this body could do. They were losing ground to this on-fire church. A man named Saul championed the opposition. He was a Christian hunter. His name would intimidate even the most loyal Christian.

Although physical death was a part of the opposition's goals, the weapons were forged in the heart. Saul viewed himself as a defender of truth and God's way. This while at the same time participating in the death of Christians.

It may sound foreign to our free ears. Surely someone would defend the believer. Of course, the church was defended, but not always in the way of flesh and blood. God's way was victory through a simple introduction. That introduction was for Saul to meet Christ Jesus the savior, crucified, risen again, and alive forevermore.

Saul's conversion on the Damascus Road shows a change of heart that brought forth God's will. No longer did imagination and religion rule the day. Righteousness in word was converted into righteousness in deed.

Christ's blood did what the law could not do.

Saul's supposed blamelessness became Paul's possession and inheritance in Christ. Unfortunately, the church's foe did not give up. The same spirit that drove Saul still operates, both outside and inside the church, attempting to kill Christians.

Cloaked in an imaginary grace that includes willful disobedience and self-righteous religious ambition, the same enemy attempts to stop God's plan. This attack comes from two fronts, people who have no idea what they are doing and people who know exactly what they are doing but are doctrinally wrong.

Christians are still suffering persecution with the threat of physical harm. Christians bear that cross around the globe, suffering with Christ in the realization of the hope of glory. However, within the gates exists a different and more ominous danger.

Doctrines that distort the design of God for the church inflict great spiritual harm. Though Christians may not be fed to the lions, the lion still looks for his prey. As a master manipulator, he will even use scripture to detour souls from their life-changing faith. He will overthrow the faith of some.

Even well-meaning ministers can channel and mimic the message that kills today's Christians. How many souls are left with no escape from the actual grip of sin? How many times have we heard, "There is none righteous, our righteousness is as filthy rags, and judge not"? That, coupled with, "We're all just sinners, we sin every day, and Jesus knows my heart," actually, out of context, echoes what Satan desires every saint to believe.

One might say, well, some of those are scripture, yes, and so is "He will give his angels charge over you," which is the verse of the Holy Bible that Satan used to tempt Christ. The enemy is fine with you believing scripture out of context. The reason is that it is void of power.

Christ was crucified so that we might become the righteousness of God in him. If we are taught and believe that is only in the world to come, we fail miserably against true context. Christ was not resurrected to leave us bound to sin in this world only to deliver us from it futuristically.

Serving sin or serving Christ is a choice. God's design is for each believer to find their walk in the Spirit where the lusts of the flesh go unfulfilled. It's time to awaken to righteousness.

We can no longer allow holiness to be unusual. We cannot allow blood-bought believers to think that Christ's righteousness was not designed to be shared. We can no longer allow sound judgment to lay silent while depravity curses and mocks the one true God.

We cannot allow the "good news" of the gospel to be a resignation of the actual victory found in a relationship with God through Christ. Are we killing Christians by the type of Christianity that we practice? Do we, in essence, diminish the possibilities in our life by failing to understand Christ's calling?

Lord, help us to know your voice and follow your lead.

# Mission General Contractor

Many people struggle for purpose in life. They look for things that will fulfill those questions that we all have faced. Why am I here? What am I supposed to be doing? Am I where I should be? Others simply do what they think needs to be done in the regular throes of work and living.

This morning I thought of some of those same questions. Am I making a difference? What really matters? This morning's manna is Mission Great Commission. That's the scripture towards the end of Matthew's gospel that says to Go! Go and teach! Go and baptize! The mission is simple, whatever you have learned from the Lord, share that.

Many people seem to be paused in their spiritual progression. These types of questions have a way of bringing a sort of paralysis to our spiritual maturity. I would like to encourage you this morning to flow in what you know. If you know, Jesus saves, teach people that Jesus saves. You don't have to know the complete story before you share the beginning. As you begin to flow in the great commission, more inspiration will come.

If you know Jesus delivers, then deliver that news. Proclaim the truth that I once was lost, but now I'm found. I now have freedom where I once was bound. I am now filled where I once was empty. Whatever, what so ever the Lord has done or is doing in your life, share that. Be faithful over the first things. God will bring the rest in His time.

In secular work, a GC is the General Contractor. On a job site, there are many varying aspects of the work at hand. The GC makes sure all of those pieces of the puzzle are in place to deliver the finished project. In our spiritual work, the GC is JC. Jesus will, through His Spirit, supply to you everything that is needed to finish the work.

The best worker on a job site is one who knows their craft. The framer isn't the concrete man. The plumber isn't the electrician, but all work together for the good, for the finished product.

Teaching people what the Lord has taught you is the great commission. You may not see the value in your part, but He does. Do what you have been called to do. Go and teach.

# Beauty Is In The Eye Of The Beholder

They say that beauty is in the eye of the beholder. One of my favorite descriptives when sharing the Word of God is beautiful. I'll often say, "It's a beautiful thing," followed by some aspect of Christianity.

A Biblical truth is that the things we see are temporary, and the things we can't see are often eternal. One of the designs of Christ's teachings is that we would see clearly. While the world is represented by blindness, spirituality is based on seeing by faith.

Jesus shared with us that in seeing him, we actually saw the Father. Of course, we also saw in him the fullness of God's spirit.

I've often thought of what it must have been like to see Christ when he came.

Many saw through the baby in a manger to realize the savior and king. Others saw through the reasoning child to see the wisdom that only comes from above. Finally, those closest to him saw the son of God and beheld the Lamb of God that takes away our sins.

Looking back can cause us to be blinded to the present. We often imagine that we would have behaved differently than Adam and Eve, doubting Thomas or denying Peter. However, sometimes it seems as if we have not seen as clearly as we imagine.

The proof of our profession must be in the present. The truth is, we have everything we need to be faithful. We struggle to rise in reality to our imagination of spiritual clarity.

We live in exciting times, yet many cannot see the harvest that is ready. The world is saturated in the oil of ministry. The Church is engaged in proportions unparalleled in human history. Yet is that what we see?

We must look beyond the nightly news, the unfaithfulness of others, and our own personal failures. We must behold Him. We must see Him in the now. We need faith now.

The analogies of the Bible paint a pretty picture of the Bride and Body of Christ. We need to see the Christ of today's mission. Lord, let us see ourselves and others clearly. Let us see your beauty and glory in those around us and in the mirror.

# No Fear

John 16:33 KJV — These things I have spoken unto you, that in me ye might have peace. In the world ye shall have tribulation: but be of good cheer; I have overcome the world.

John 14:1 Don't let your heart be troubled.

Forever hope conquerors temporary anxiety.

John 16:1 These things have I spoken unto you, that ye should not be offended.

Last week I was encouraged by the word and direction I felt I needed to share Sunday. I wasn't sure whether just to post it to social media or just preach it Sunday morning. Well, the word is one that is valid in all seasons, so I thought I would share it here.

Sometimes the most basic of truths are overlooked. This causes believers to struggle unnecessarily. I was thinking of the truth of Psalms 23, where a believer states, "I will fear no evil." What would your life look like without fear?

The verses that are posted above give remedy to life's ills. The truth is that the world is full of tribulation, suffering, persecution, etc. However, through the power of a risen Christ, we, too, can overcome.

My goal is to empower each of you with the truth that you don't have to worry. You don't have to fear. You don't have to be offended or live in any one of these states.

The truth is that God has given you the power to have a sound mind in the face of the world's system. Don't let your heart be troubled. When we are warned of perilous times, we should not be surprised when they come. Our reaction to our circumstances must be controlled.

We have the power to let things get out of control, just as we have the power to keep things within the prescribed boundaries that these scriptures offer. Don't let the world dictate to you your state of mind.

If allowed to, our minds create imaginations that will rob us of peace, joy, and the power of the Holy Ghost. It's not that God's power is not available; it's that we leave it on the shelf while the world forces its way upon us. If allowed to, reality will rob us of the same.

DON'T LET IT.

# Hitting The Mark Of Your Greater Self

Have you ever heard the excuse for someone's behavior, "Well, that's just her," or, "That's just the way he is?" I'm not sure that there has ever been a greater cover than to settle for such a lack.

Throughout the years of ministry, we have encountered many personality types. There are the outspoken, withdrawn, timid, and zealous, every type imaginable. However, there is nothing new under the sun.

With the experience of meeting people, I had questioned before how did they get to this point in life that way? I suppose the message of a better way has been delayed. Christ provides a better way. In fact, He is the better way.

I wonder if we often miss our greater self by settling for that's just the way it is. Well, if something is lacking, it's not God's fault; it is yours and mine.

I'm not speaking as one who has mastered every personality quirk of myself but as one who believes in a Christ that can help with the change. I refuse to settle on the wrong side of the river if there's a promise of a better way waiting on the other shore.

If our "Christian" conversation is filled with gossip and slander, there is a better way. If our daily life includes extended times of separation from God in the varying aspects of business, there is a better way. If blatant and unrepentant sin is constantly present, there is a better way.

Do not miss your best self at this time of your life. Everything that we need to walk worthy is available. Whether we need grace and mercy, or revelation and inspiration, it is available. If we have settled for less, let it be realized in every aspect of our lives.

Let God arise in your person. Let His enemies be scattered in your life. May you walk at this moment as the greatest you have ever been. It's okay to be you, just be a Godly you.

# Lost And Found

Part of the blessing of having been raised in church is the old hymns that often come to mind. I was thinking of a couple of those yesterday and got tickled at my childhood memories. One of those songs was "Bringing in the Sheaves," which I thought said sheep. Well, either one works.

Another song I mistook was "Rescue the Perishing." I'm not sure if it was my hearing or their singing, but I thought they were saying rescue the parachutes! The perishing and the sheaves were unfamiliar terms. I laugh about my misunderstandings now, but there's a point to be made.

Our lives are filled with relationships and people who are lost and don't know it. Without the knowledge of Jesus Christ, those souls will perish. That harvest of souls is what the gospel message is all about.

God has chosen you to be a part of the last days' harvest that will bring in the sheaves, the perishing, and the sheep safe into the fold. I say the last days because we are closer now than we have ever been to the coming of the Lord. If the fields were ripe in the first century, they must be plentiful now.

The call for laborers is still in effect. The risk still exists. There is a heaven to be gained and a hell to shun down. Will you help us win the lost until all are found?

# Confirmation

I love it when a plan comes together. Throughout the years of ministry, one thing has remained a constant source of encouragement. Receiving the Holy Spirit's sweet confirmation has always been a blessing.

You have heard it said, "Birds of a feather flock together, "well, the same is true for those who have set their affections on things above. God has a way of reminding us that we are not alone and also that we are on the right track.

It happens when you surround yourself with God's people, whose purpose and mission are the same as yours. It happens through shared thoughts, scriptures, and songs. The Lord has often sent a simple word from a brother or sister in the faith to bring that blessed assurance.

It doesn't have to be contrived or imagined. It happens to those whose steps are being ordered by the Lord. It happens when you open your Bible to an exact scripture. It happens when your personal study mirrors that of shared study in the same circle.

It happens when an uncoordinated Sunday lesson matches the morning's message and scriptures. It happens when the song choice matches the cry of our hearts.

When two become one, we all mind the same things and begin to function as a body in unison rather than being just separated individuals. It's as if God says yes and amen to you personally and to those who journey alongside you.

Thank you, Jesus, for caring enough to let me know you hear me when I pray and that my future and present are safe in your hands.

# There Is Jesus!

Have you ever been mistaken for Jesus? A few years ago, a young family began coming to church. Their children were very young, and after a few years, attendance was a vital part of their lives.

As a pastor, I lived in the parsonage next door and would make my way over to the church at service times to open up. One day that seemingly mundane task turned into a teachable moment and a blessing.

On that particular occasion, as I walked to the church, the family pulled in at that exact moment. The baby of the couple exclaimed, "There's Jesus!" when he saw me. Of course, the mom let the child know the difference, but he had learned that he had been coming to God's house for a while and was also learning about Jesus every time.

I was both humbled and elated. To think that I had been mistaken for Jesus was something that I could not remember happening. It made me pause and reflect on what it really means to be like Him.

I was just being a doorkeeper. You may think you are just visiting. You may think that you are just doing what the right thing to do is. However, there are aspects of our lives that reflect Jesus.

When we are kind, forgiving, and loving, it reminds people of our savior. To some, we remind them of a crucified Christ. To others, we make them realize that Jesus is alive.

I often reflect on the words of the Lord about doing good to the least and ministering to the body as He would. When our actions are those of the hands and feet of the body of Christ, there is Jesus. When we are overly generous, there is Jesus. When we are faithful, there is Jesus. When we love the unlovable or forgive the unforgivable, there is Jesus.

I hope that someone might say of our deeds, "that is the most Christlike thing I have ever seen." Jesus said that if you'd seen Him, you had seen the Father. I pray that the world might see Jesus in us, the hope of glory.

# Giving The Gift Of Yourself

Will a man rob God? There are many who will read no further. The scriptural reference here pertains to financial faithfulness. The unfaithful are automatically offended. However, the robbery of which I speak is one of a deeper level, so please read on.

Instead of missing gifts to the altar, I would like to address those that come from the altar. Years ago, I was appointed to a church. There was a church building and a parsonage, but it seemed like the people were missing. You know, here is the door, here is the steeple, open the door, where are all of the people?

After many messages, I had a friend visit. He came from a larger church. I spoke, and he responded afterwards and said to me, "Man, you preached like there was a crowd!" Well, to me, there was a crowd, we had gathered about thirty souls. When you first start out with three people, thirty people seem more like a crowd. Yet, even with thirty, there were plenty of seats left open. Those open and empty seats meant open and empty positions.

I began calling those missing members. Not on the phone but rather in the spirit. I had friends praying, and God sent them in from all directions. I preached to the empty seats, "Seats be filled."

Lately, I have been thinking about what we rob God and others of when we are MIA. That means missing in action. As a shepherding habit, I always look for those who are missing. Are they ok? Are they sick? Have they flown the coop? This is not to address simply missing church. It is about what the church is missing from you.

God has given us gifts, talents, abilities, time, and breath. Have we robbed Him by taking what he has given and repurposing it? Is the body of Christ missing the part that is you?

If God can be robbed, some must rethink sovereignty versus free will. It is not that God has not given, but rather that many have taken without proper allocation. It is much like a misappropriation of funds. It is kind of like taking something meant for the church and either hiding it away or using it inappropriately.

The church is often looked at as an object rather than as an us. We think our missing part will not matter. What if every gift and calling went unused and unanswered? Where, then, would we, the church be? Thank God for those who faithfully fulfill their part. We are waiting for you.

# After The Shout

The Old Testament is full of lessons beneficial for today. I was recently reminded of a people and a time from the scripture when things didn't go quite as planned. The story circles around a battle and a shout, but no victory.

In fact, there are a few instances of the same type of circumstances leading to a less-than-desirable outcome. Just after Jericho fell, victory became elusive. Disobedience caused a pause in Israel's triumph. A people blessed by God were sidelined by behavior.

I wish that this lesson could have been learned after one defeat. However, the Biblical track record of captivity and losses tells a different story. A story that, from generation to generation, still needs to be understood.

God is, of course, worthy of all praise, glory, and honor that we could ever give. You can give God the glory and still not get the victory. Do you think the Israelites were thankful for the falling walls of Jericho that came down with a shout? Of course, but the next battle showed that the walk after the win can adversely affect outcomes.

The time I was thinking about was around the era of Elijah. Israel's disobedience was common, and so was the knowledge that God was able and worthy. The story progresses to the battlefield, where God's people began to feel defeated.

As a remedy for their defeat, they chose to fetch the Ark, oh, what a shout! It caused the enemy to stop and think. The problem was that victory comes from obedience, not the shout. The Ark of the Covenant ends up being captured by the Philistines. In this case, there was no victory after the shout.

In these accounts, we see that obedience to the word is greater than the sacrifice of the shout. The adherence to God's marching orders is needed before, during, and after any battle. Without that, the exclamation, even of the greatness of God, is just noise.

When you fight, worship, pray, or live, let it be in the footsteps of the way in which we have been led by Christ and His word. His instructions are paramount to the imaginations, feelings, and preconceived notions of men.

My desire is that we walk in victory in every aspect of life. What might seem impossible to you now is possible through God. Trust and Obey; there is no other way.

# Check

In preparation for my next sermon, I have been thinking about the game of chess. I used to play more than I do now and was once pretty good at the game. I began having thoughts about life and the kingdoms represented in relation to the pieces on the board.

Of course, there's only one true king. I suppose identifying that role is a given. What about the other kingdom pieces? Take, for example, the pawn. Many view being a pawn in a strictly negative light. I suppose it depends on whether you are playing or being played.

The pawn, as the smallest piece on the board, seems insignificant. However, they provide the front line of the fray and can prove to be the most pivotal part of the end game.

In relation to the kingdom, I see the pawn as the believer. Though many might see them as lesser or even expendable, I see them as the core. They are the kingdom; they are the masses. They serve with purpose. Think of the value of the martyrs.

Knowing the game, of course, means knowing each piece, each purpose, and the way each works. I thought of the rook as the deacons. They are positioned for order. They represent definite boundaries, the straight and the narrow. They hold the whole together.

If I were to assign or ascribe the knight, maybe it would be the evangelist or prophet. They certainly represent the most unconventional movement on the field. Just when you think you have them figured out, their direction might change and surprise you. They can transcend other fixed positions like no other.

That would bring us to the bishop. Slicing through the board's turmoil, they cover a great distance. They provide the closest support for the king. They represent the authority of the kingdom and the abilities only held by themselves. The bishop is the bishop.

Many see the queen as the most important. Some players lose all heart when their queen is lost, and most of the time, rightfully so. Who is the queen of the kingdom? I see it as the church, the bride of Christ. What a powerful force.

The church rallies the believers, places in order the deacons, sets forth the evangelist and ordains the bishop. It is the unity that the church provides that brings home victory for the king.

Well, there you have it. May every time you play again, you think about what is really going on.

# Make A Joyful Noise

I'm going to sing in the middle of my storm.

This morning, my prayer time turned into the all-request hour of song. Old and new songs alike came one right after another.

The fact that the world is on fire does not stop my song. The fact that I can't sing does not stop my song. You see, my song comes from a deeper well than anything this world knows or can understand. My song springs up in spite of!

Like an overflowing stream of joy, my heart tells a story. It's a love song. It's a life story. It's the mix of my past, present, and future in the light of Christ. Circumstances are sometimes designed to steal or stop your song. Storms, trials, and failures all can align to keep you from the heart's cry to tell that story.

There is a contagious aspect to allowing your soul to glorify the Lord, to magnify His name, and to rise above. Before you know it, questions will come from others about your song and your story, which in turn will lead to your testimony. You will eventually point those souls to Calvary. Just think, your song can impact someone's eternity.

My encouragement today is for you to sing! Make that joyful noise. There is a song inside of you waiting to break out!

# Morning Manna Or Yesterday's Meat

Are any of you old enough to the point where your body creaks? Maybe with the change of the weather, there is a little aching? The point is we know when our joints are hurting. It makes one appreciate when they are working properly! I've had a scripture on my mind for the last few weeks and just thought I would share a little about the subject. Coming from Ephesians, the 4th chapter, there is a verse that speaks about the supply that comes from every joint to build the body.

The intricacy of the body is amazing. Every part is doing its part. It all flows together as was purposed. This is descriptive of the body of Christ, the church. You are the body of Christ, and each of you is designed to fulfill a function.

As the children's song says, the bones need to hear the Word of the Lord and come together. The knee bone is connected to the leg bone. Well, it's supposed to be connected. When our joints are out of place, our body suffers. If any of you have had a dislocated knee, shoulder, or finger, you know what I'm talking about. If you've had inflammation in a joint, a ruptured or bulging disc, you know what I'm talking about.

The joints are the connections that make the bodywork. Without them, we are alone and dry. In this analogy, they represent the relationships we have with one another. Watching a church attempt to function without the needful things those proper relationships supply is painful. It can range from a limp to total paralysis.

After years of abuse, my elbow has needed a little help to function properly. Some of you may have benefited from a little extra fluid. It is strange, but some have been sidelined by too much fluid. The perfect function of the body is a harmonic event. Do you think the Lord knows what His body needs? Of course, He does. What He needs is for you to do your part in Him to supply the next part with what they need.

The isolation of a believer is as painful to watch as a dislocated joint. A few years ago, my wife's knee went out of joint and would not go back in. We were on the brink of an emergency room visit. It was extremely painful for her. It was killing me to see her suffer. After realizing that there had to be a way to fix this, I simply mimicked what a doctor would do and was able to reset her knee. Folks, we have a relationship with the great physician. If we hear His remedy, we will live and live a life of abundance.

Is the body of Christ benefiting from the relationships you have forged, or are you sidelined by the numerous conditions of ill?

Hey, bones! Hear the Word of the Lord! Come together! Supply what is needed for us all to grow in love and power. If you have been forgiven, forgive! If you have been gifted, GIVE! To the ear, HEAR! To the feet, GO! To the eye, SEE! To the hand HOLD FAST! To the knee, BOW! To the tongue, CONFESS and PROFESS! An exceeding great army waits with patience for your participation.

# The Beautiful Feet Of Jesus

If we fast forward to the end of the story, the gospel, and the Bible, we will find the triumphant feet of Jesus. Where death is defeated and we enjoy eternal glory. It's not hard to find beauty there.

Blessed are those who get it. You know the ones who walk by faith now. Those who have mobilized for hope's sake. Trying to find your way? Try finding the beauty at the feet of Jesus.

There are many busy people. Most of us are very busy, but are you busy with the Father's business? The gospel shares the story of two sisters. One was cumbered about with busyness; the other found something different, learning at the feet of Jesus.

I can imagine the stories, the truth, the depth, and the beauty that she must have experienced. It's not that Martha was bad for being busy, but that Mary had found that good and precious part, which was hearing the Word of the Lord.

Forgiveness is found at the feet of Jesus. Sum up every sin you have committed. Multiply that by those of the whole world. Know that your sins can be forgiven. I think of my own tears shed at the altar, at Jesus's feet. How beautiful is that cleansing?

Somehow, I now understand the woman who cried at His feet enough to wash them. I know the feeling of needing forgiveness and getting it. Is there anything that you need to lay there?

Humility is found at the feet of Jesus. My thoughts often go to the moment Jesus washed His disciples' feet. He did so as an example that we would do the same. It's not about the act itself but the pride-breaking aspect of humbling yourself. Without that deep sense of humility, we do not have a part in God's plan.

It's beautiful when brothers and sisters can fellowship, forgive, and learn more about Him. As the body of Christ, I can certainly see how the feet of the Church can also hold that same beauty.

"How beautiful upon the mountains are the feet of him that bringeth good tidings, that publisheth peace; that bringeth good tidings of good, that publisheth salvation; that saith unto Zion, Thy God reigneth!"

There was a man whose calling took him to the body of Christ. Joseph of Arimathea prepared Jesus for his burial. I want you to imagine how his calling now was to wash the feet of Jesus. I can feel the emotion of every move. Wiping away the dust and blood, he revealed the beautiful feet of Jesus.

Who of us would not have done the same? Knowing now who Christ is, we would all volunteer for that job. With that in mind, see Jesus in your brother and your sister, and as He said to, do likewise. Your learning, your forgiveness, and your humility will serve to reveal the beautiful feet of the body of Christ.

# The Bloody Feet Of Jesus

My vision is one of seeing Christ's feet stained with a mixture of dust and blood. One where nails have pierced Him. His precious blood has run down his body from the crown of thorns and the stripes to the bloody feet of Jesus.

If you are spiritual, this is for you. When I say spiritual, I mean, of course, redeemed by Christ's blood. We come from a long line of warriors, victorious warriors. We are the followers of the Lord of the battle.

I imagine what Abraham's feet looked like as he returned from the slaughter of the kings. Or, what did Samson's feet look like after he finished wielding that jawbone? Or, even David, as he removed the giant's head.

The bloody feet of Jesus took him through the stations of the cross and ultimately to His crucifixion. However, we know that the story does not end there. We know that those feet secured for us eternal victory.

As the body of Christ, we must know that spiritual warfare is still going on. Though Abraham, Samson, and David were precursors, Christ's sacrifice engages us as his body in that spiritual battle.

The future holds a glorious future for the body of Christ, but there remains a fight to be fought. It is a battle for the souls of humanity. Though Christ's work of sacrifice was finished on the cross, our calling is to engage the enemy in a similar manner. In doing so, the feet of the body of Christ will be bloody from the battle.

We are told to take up our cross, fight the good fight, and understand the connection to His suffering. We are told that our feet are to be shod, which I will equate to "strap on your boots." Jesus has called us to warfare, and He has equipped and enabled us to win.

"And your feet shod with the preparation of the gospel of peace" The Ephesians reference to the Christian's armor uses the KJV word "shod" covering the feet. The word actually means, in legal terms, that your feet become deadly weapons.

Can you hear the conqueror's tread? Spiritually we tread on serpents, scorpions, and all the power of the enemy. Eventually, the enemy of death will be under the feet of Christ's body. Ultimately, every aspect of evil will fall and be the spoils of victory under our feet.

The church's mission now has boots on the ground. The battle is the Lord's, but the fight is yours. Are you prepared? Are you engaged in this battle? Truly, when the battle is over, we shall wear a crown, but it will be won by the bloody feet of Jesus both then and now.

# The Dirty Feet of Jesus

If you are a part of any type of hands-on church work, you know that sometimes it gets tough. It takes a special kind of commitment to continue to suffer the way church workers do and then to continue the mission. Sometimes, the phrase glutton for punishment comes to mind.

While preparing to speak at our ministry's leadership weekend, I was impressed to share a boots on the ground, getting down and dirty type of message. Those two phrases were actually voiced by a couple of brothers who were fine-tuned to the Spirit.

We know that we are the body of Christ. I know many often quiz themselves about what part of the body they might be. While others may see themselves as a more beautiful part, I'll be satisfied with just being the feet. In fact, even the dirty feet.

The thought behind that notion comes from the way that Jesus walked the dusty roads with a down-to-earth ministry that got His feet dirty.

I was thinking about the woman who touched the hem of his garment with the crowd, the dirt, and the dust during that event. Or better still, the woman who washed Jesus's feet with her tears and hair. Sounds like a fairly dirty business to me.

We are not to be of those who are fearful of touching or being touched. Jesus called out religious onlookers who decried His allowing the woman to even touch Him.

Jesus set the servitude example. He washed the feet of His disciples and encouraged them to do likewise. We like to think of ministry as neat and clean. It is not. It is a dusty, dirty road.

The drug addicts are not clean. The adulterous are not clean. Traversing the highways, byways, and hedges are not ways to stay clean. Sure, you can keep your shoes shiny if you stay in the church, but the church's work is in the dirt.

The church's work is out there. It's to the halt, the maimed, and the withered. The church's mission includes the poor, the hungry, and the naked. Our mission includes the oppressed, depressed, and possessed. Not many wise, not many noble have accepted this truth.

The purist of religion includes affliction. The afflicted require interaction and involvement. Ministry calls us to the other side of the tracks. It takes us to the less-than-desirable places. The feet of Jesus engage people where they are.

You can remain clean on the outside, but in doing so, you miss the mission at hand. This results in those who would be touched, cleansed, or changed remaining dead in their sins.

Religion on the outside leaves the "dirty" work to others. If you will be Christlike, your feet will get dirty. Surround yourself with people who are not afraid of the work. Be the body, even if it is the dirty feet of Jesus.

# Dead End

Our church's sign for Crossroads Chapel is a road sign depicting an intersection. The driving thought behind the sign is that everyone faces those times in life when choices must be made.

Should I stay or should I go? Should I pursue this relationship? Should I...? You fill in the blank. The church is purposed to help with life's choices which ultimately points souls to Calvary.

As a part of ministry, you come to realize that thought processes dictate direction. As a part of biblical understanding, it is the control of those processes that lead to victory. You can choose what you think about.

The scriptural injunction to think about those spiritually healthy things is a great kingdom key. Focus is key. I often use the Dead-End Road sign to help people control their own thoughts.

It's easy to be distracted. I have heard the rumble strips on the roadside many times. They sound off to let you know that you are not paying the best of attention. The message is you can do better, and you are better.

If we ignore the warning signs in our thought processes, we will find ourselves at the bitter end of an unnecessary journey. Anger, depression, anxiety, and the like are often the result of not paying as close attention to what we are thinking about as we should.

As a believer and a disciple of Christ, our focus should be on those things which are spiritually beneficial. Identifying avenues of thought that are not good is the way we begin to reign in those detrimental trips.

When we are traveling and we see a sign that says Dead End we turn around at the first available opportunity. In your mind, you should do the same thing. There is no sense in going to the end of the dead end to make sure. You will find yourself captured by your thoughts rather than capturing your thoughts.

At the first sign of an unhealthy line of thinking, turn around. Don't allow imaginative thoughts to control you and override the fact that you can control them. Through the power that God gives, you can have the stability that is needed for your success.

You would have to admit that there are plenty of things to think about. Choose those high-road thoughts that lead to spiritual strength. Think about those things.

# Living In The Light Of The Keyhole

Life is beautiful. Life is undeniable. We open our eyes in life. We open our eyes, and light shows us life. The design is purposeful.

I was sitting looking at an old country door. From my vantage point, I could see the light outside through the keyhole. After attempting to spider-proof our family cabin, I was taken aback by the opening. My thought was that if light can get through, so can... well, you know.

I began to think of Christ as the door to light and life. He is real. He is there. He is the only reason that we live. Light and life are waiting on the other side of that door. However, so many people only see what they see because of the keyhole.

The life they live and the breath they breathe comes from the other side. The measured and limited life now experienced, we experience by design. Humanity lives life through the light of the keyhole.

I view life as an opportunity to know more. With every road trip, we enjoy something new. Something that we may not have seen before. When asked about ambitions in life, many people's answer is, "I want to see the world." I want that too, but I want more.

I don't just want to live; I want to embrace the meaning of life. If the key is available, if the door can be opened, then that is what I want. All of us have a view of life through the keyhole. True Christians see life through the opened door.

In the chest beside our cabin's door was a skeleton key. Actually, two keys, one old and one new, and I tried both. I was pleasantly surprised that the old rusty key still fit and turned the lock. In life, each of you has a door and a key. You can live life without ever knowing Jesus, but that is not life's design.

God has given everyone a measure of faith. A certain quantity of knowing. To the right of the cabin's door is a bookcase. The keys to life's questions sit on its shelf. The Bible is called the good book. It's filled with keys that will take you to what waits on the other side.

There's more to life than just living.

# Turtle On A Fencepost

Gee, the turtle, what an example.

I have heard it said that if you ever see a turtle sitting on the fence post, he had a little help getting there. The truth tells us that in the last few days, people will become very self-focused, loving themselves, proud of themselves, and boasting about what they have accomplished. Well, it seems that that time is close.

Others retreat into the "I cannot" syndrome. They are self-absorbed, just not in a positive manner. Instead of being proud and boasting, they diminish themselves with excuses which eventually paralyzes them from success in any aspect.

Humbling the proud and exalting the humble is God's business. His hands work the work like a potter would do a vessel. Now, we are His hands. We have been given much.

Today, I accept the truth that if it were not for God's hands, I would be nothing. If it were not also for Godly hands, I would be nothing. He formed and fashioned me in my mother's womb. Then, my parents and Godly people shaped and molded me to know my maker.

If it were not for this appointed system, we would be nothing. Without Him, nothing was created. Without His hands on earth, we would also be hopeless. Today, I thank God for breath and life. I thank Him for mothers and fathers, brothers and sisters, and the Godly wives, sons, and daughters.

Without God and those who follow on to know him, where would you be? Today, remember in Him that we live and breathe and have what we have. With His earthly hands and within the arms of His fellowship, we have helped to accomplish the tasks set before us. Thank Him and someone today who has helped you along your way.

If you need help, it's available.

# Dead Letterist

The Bible cannot save you. It is not a book of magical recipes for spiritual success. In fact, at times, it diminishes itself by its own verses. Much like Christ pointing to and honoring the Father.

One of the most obvious examples is 2 Cor. 3:6, where the letter kills, but the Spirit gives life. Of course, this is speaking of God's Holy Spirit and what is referred to in scripture as the Holy Ghost. We could also say the Spirit of truth, the comforter, the spirit of God, of the Lord, of the Lord Jesus Christ.

That one Spirit is the eternal Spirit. Without His call, you cannot know the Lord. Of course, many profess the name of Jesus or Christianity but do so without that Spirit.

It is that Spirit that brings life to the letter, the scripture, and the Bible. Without His illumination, revelation, His voice, the Bible itself will be illusive to our understanding.

There are many dead letterist. They reverence the Bible. They pick over the finest of points. They use it religiously for themselves and for others. Sounds great, right? Except, without the Spirit, much of what is practiced in such a manner only deafens the ear of the hearer. They learn, but they never truly know.

They say, "Want to hear from God? Read the Bible." However, it's not that simple. What if the first verses they read show them that there is more to God than the finite aspects of the Scripture? What if they are introduced to a God that hears and speaks?

Dead letterist desire to reduce God to something they can see, read, and fully understand. If it's not written, it's discarded as less. If someone says, "God told me," they are ridiculed, scoffed at, or mocked.

I understand that not everyone who says God said represents the truth or the Spirit's leading. However, saying God does not still speak is one of the most detrimental teachings a seeker can find.

2 Cor. 3:15-18 says that there is a heart condition that keeps people from seeing even when they see. This means they read, but the spiritual aspect eludes them. The truth is that the Spirit's input is needed to bring those truths to light.

Sometimes it's semantics that separates us regarding God speaking. Sometimes it's the death that works even within the pages of the Bible that blinds the eye and deafens the ear of the heart.

The Bible has yet to be translated into every language. Yet the Bible says there is no speech or language where His truth is not heard and that the Heavens declare the Glory of God. The scripture itself says that it is not possible to contain all of the truth of God's word.

That means truth exists outside of the written text. As a historical word, how many things are true, they happened, but there is no possible way to record every truth. In the same manner, the nature of God, the revelation of Jesus Christ, and His creative essence cannot be summed up in a limited fashion.

The Bible does not need you to prop it up. Used unskillfully, it can do more damage than good. I have experienced what it is like to have the truth of the Bible without the Spirit that gives it light.

It's like religion without a relationship. Of course, there is a religion that is pure, but without the Spirit of truth, truth is itself dampened. The Bible is truth. How to navigate that truth is by being Spirit-led.

The Bible says so.

John 16:13. Howbeit when he, the Spirit of truth, is come, he will guide you into all truth: for he shall not speak of himself; but whatsoever he shall hear, that shall he speak: and he will shew you things to come.

The Bible says the Spirit will speak. It doesn't say that He stops. Those who believe that God stopped speaking are called cessationists. They believe that once the apostles died and the Bible was written that God somehow stopped communicating with His children.

Now they say they believe that; however, in listening to their arguments, I have heard a different take. "God showed me" is very close to "God told me." I felt led, I saw something in a different light, I was inspired, the Lord revealed to me, He impressed me to, I was prompted, all show you the interactive nature of God beyond the written text.

Not one comes to the Lord without the Spirit's drawing. That calling does not end with salvation. It's a continuous interactive fellowship. A relationship. A walk in the Spirit. One where He speaks, and we hear. Speak, Lord, let your people hear.

# Quit Being A Quitter

The anatomy of "I quit." Here are some observations from the front.

As a part of a church and motorcycle ministry, I have seen my share of quitters. Having never been one, it is very frustrating to watch. It seems mostly to be based on the old adage, "If I can't have it my way, I'll just take my toys and go home."

Well, what happens when you are home? I think that brings me back to why I have never been a quitter. My church is my home, and my ministry is who I am, like a family. Of course, we have those who quit that too.

Early in pastoral ministry, we visited a family with a small son. We had our son with us, who was relatively the same age. As we sat for a visit, I watched as the child snatched from my son anything he would pick up. All the while, the parents stood idly by. We live in a generation of spoiled brats.

We deal with people daily who have never been told no. Authority, community, and organization all suffer from this self-centered, self-absorbed culture that we often foster. The response of the offender is, "I quit!"

For them, it is easier to live in the imagination than it is with everybody else. As a society, we have removed the stigma of shame even when it is applicable. We have sacrificed truth for possibilities. Meaning if we make excuses for people's behavior, maybe it will be better.

Even worse than that, maybe we can make structural or behavioral changes that will keep people from quitting. There is no amount of healthy change that will assuage a bully or self-absorbed individual who would rather have it their way or no way at all.

I don't mean that there is never a time for a healthy transition. Sometimes that may mean I quit. Such as, I quit putting up with your abuse, or I quit allowing my emotions to override my spiritual sensibilities, etc.

Find a spine and a bit of humility. The combination is a strong one. In life and ministry, we run into our fair share of people who need both. Don't allow the "I quitters" to rule another day, and don't let it be you.

# Why Not Today

If you ever will.

There is a sense of urgency stirring in God's people. Having a network of dear brothers and sisters, I have heard in them and from them a definite shift. It's getting late, spiritually speaking.

There have always been those who scoff at the notions of end-time events. I often cover my bases of beliefs by saying it is definitely closer than it's ever been. Even if Christ's coming, I often say it is more likely that you go to meet Him.

This morning I awake to a fresh sense of the unfolding hands of time. I should be sleeping, but I'm watching, I'm waiting, and I am believing. I am calling to those who will hear. To those who have a spiritual ear to hear the Spirit, come.

Do not delay. Come and see. Taste and see. Experience and know. God is good, and time, as we know it, is slipping away.

If one hears or sees, I will at least have sounded a trumpet. I will have done my part to speak what I hear.

If you have been waiting, today is the day of salvation. Call on the Lord. He will show you things you did not know. Call on Him and be saved.

If you ever were going to change, to be faithful, to turn from the world and turn to Christ, please hear what the Spirit is saying to you. Come all of you who are experiencing heaviness. There is change available. Come. The invitation is timed. Now is the best option. Don't delay.

# No Puny Grapes

They say that those who refuse to learn from the past are doomed to repeat it. Being somewhat of a student of history, I enjoy the truths and lessons that can be learned from it. Knowing things and processes of days gone by can benefit you in the now.

On our recent trip through an antique store, I noticed a piece in a cabinet. I immediately knew what it was. It was mislabeled by someone who did not know the truth; they did not know the whole story. This piece was labeled "Hunters Return."

The figures represented so much more. It was the grapes of Eshcol. It was an artist's rendering of the fruit of the promised land. When Moses sent the spies into the land, they returned with this cluster of grapes.

Upon further inspection, I noticed the carving still had a tag on it from the Holy Land. The story relayed through the art was a scripture that I had preached before. The message was entitled "No Puny Grapes."

This caused me to reflect and realize there are many who still do not know the truth. They do not know the benefits of serving the Lord. They could know. The Word contains the plan. It's there; the examples and lessons of the past are there. They exist to impact your present.

I see a lesson in life. When we look at people or even ourselves, do we, too, mislabel? Do we fail to understand the plenty that waits for us? Do we settle for what the world sees? Do we wait on the banks of the river, never knowing what is there just on the other side?

I challenge you to learn from the Word what God has planned, what God has done, and what God has designed for your life. There is a great harvest that waits. The Lord is waiting patiently for you.

Yes, the piece came home with me!

# The Middle Of The Road

As a young minister, I had many questions. I wanted to do things correctly. I wanted to function in such a way that would be right in God's eyes. I found myself asking my grandfather about a host of issues. I was fortunate to have a voice of reason.

In all of my "What about this" and "What about that" quizzes, one piece of advice that he shared with me still stands out to me today. He said, "Son, there will be people on the left and people on the right; get in the middle of the road and keep your eyes on Jesus."

In that moment, I felt that the advice was rather simplistic. As I have journeyed, I have come to the realization that this was wise counsel.

You see, life has ditches, and those ditches are designed to entrap you. Many people operate too close to the ditch. For some reason or another, their focus shifts ever so slightly from Christ. The end result is devastating. The scripture describes the condition as a type of blindness.

People are often right in their own eyes. Religious people and sinful people alike have simply chosen a side. Both sides have the same peril. It is as if a pendulum swings from one extreme to the other while the truth resides in the center.

Both left and right reject the truth. Just as Jesus was rejected by men, you will be as well. The religious attempt to persuade to a position of false piety while the wicked call to overindulgence. This results in the blind attempting to lead the blind.

I recently heard another testimony about a "minister's" rejection of a traveler. The traveler needed kindness. What he received was false doctrine. Instead of Christ-like qualities, he was judged.

Yet another account of a soul on life's road came to me in the form of a prayer request. Needing direction and acceptance, that soul veered from sound doctrine headlong into the open arms of sin's delusion.

Both were off track. They were simply on the opposite side of the road. One stands to accept you only if you reject the truth for a pretty lie. The other blesses your ugly lies along with their own.

Now the middle of the road sounds like the place to be. Jesus, by His Holy Spirit, will lead you into all truth. There are people attempting to distract you from both sides. Listen to the voice of the Shepherd.

# Progress

When I was a child, before an individual could become a member of the church, the elders would say that one needed to have a vision of the church. I would like to take a moment and break down how one's vision can progress and mature.

When a person drives by a church or hears about a church, it is THAT church. Maybe they have seen or heard of it before. Perhaps they thought of trying it out. However, the unknown makes it THAT church. Of course, one could also try it with blinders, not really seeing, have a so-so or not-so-good experience, and it remains, "Oh, THAT church."

When a person comes in and frequents the services and realizes the benefits, their understanding will change from THAT church to THIS church. They ask questions. They quiz the leaders and members, "Does this church believe x, y, and z?". From the inside, the perspective is a little more accurate. It's no longer that church but THIS church.

At some point in the deepening understanding, an individual realizes that they are THIS church, and to them, it becomes MY church. An investment and commitment breed ownership. They contribute, take part, and want what is best for their church.

As the vision expands, a God thing takes place. You see, God actually adds individuals to the whole. We may think we have some control and we do our best, but it's His business. At some point, the MY church perspective becomes an OUR church perspective because one understands that they are not alone. The church is a family. Fathers and mothers, sons and daughters, brothers and sisters where all share the same calling.

The final aspect of the calling is the revelation of what the church really is. Revelation brings the clearest of vision. One sees the church in the light of God's word. The church is the bride of Christ. So, all along the way, our comprehension has developed to the reality that it is HIS church. He purchased and purposed the church.

It's not that any partial understanding is off or misguided but rather a symbol of the deepening and developing grasp of God's plan. His plan is to add to the church such as should be added. His plan is for HIS church to stand the test of time and come out of this world victorious, triumphant, and glorious.

The best news is that this will come to pass. Where are you? Are you in? Do you have a vision of and a passion for HIS church?

I hope you make it to church this Sunday.

# The Response

My thoughts this morning run to the many varying responses to Christ by the individuals who encountered him in the Biblical narrative. The situations and circumstances of these meetings seem to be perfectly and randomly orchestrated by an unseen order. Of course, we know that to be God.

Whether it be a woman by a well, a short man in a tree, a prophet, or a prostitute, Jesus met these people where they were.

And at the moment, what seems like chance turns into the divine. Today, salvation visits the house. Today, healing visits the house. Today, the resurrection visits the house.

2 Corinthians 1:20 reminds us that in Christ, all the promises of God are yes and amen. The promises of God are real and are there to be realized. What is your response?

What is your response to God's promises? Do you doubt and need more detail? So did a disciple named Thomas. Thomas' response to a resurrected savior was one of "I will believe it when I see it." In that spiritual moment, Jehovah Jireh shows Thomas the wounds of the crucifixion.

John 20:25-29

God provides a life-changing proposal, and the response is on you. In this particular case, Thomas had not seen what others had already experienced. He was unsure. He was uncertain. At that moment, his mind and his heart were broken, but God has a response to the broken. He comes near and presents us with his presence, which then necessitates our response. Jesus offered his hand and his heart. Thomas' faith and lack thereof is turned into a realization of God's promise in Christ, which is yes and amen.

Jesus doesn't stop at Thomas' uncertainties. He ventures into today, from the pages of the Scripture, and addresses your faith. By sight, Thomas transitioned from doubt into faith. Jesus says your faith can be even better than one who stood next to him, whose eyes beheld and witnessed. Yes, your faith can be stronger. It depends on your response.

The varying circumstances in which Christ operates are as vast as the spectrum of people that humanity's population represents. In this display, you find yourself. You find yourself a recipient of God's calling. You hear, what do you say? We often find ourselves in similar situations to biblical reality.

Maybe you are like the man who believed but needed help with his belief. Jesus found something precious in that profound honesty, and the man received deliverance for his child. Jesus had presented the opportunity if you can believe all things are possible. The response was one of a certain uncertainty. I believe, Jesus, help my unbelief.

I'm sure we can identify. Many times, even in Christ, there are moments that are less than clear. We know God is able. We believe Christ cares, but we struggle to manifest his promises. You know his promise to cast your care upon him, his promise to never leave you, and his promise of a certain future.

What is your response to his presence? Thomas was one way when he thought Jesus really wasn't there. However, at the revelation of Jesus in the present, his response to the truth changes. The man with the problematic child was in his presence but needed a deeper understanding to realize the victory that was available.

At the presentation of Jesus, the woman with the issue of blood stood out in the crowd by faith. Her response to Jesus was a certain reaching out and touching that she was certain would bring change. If we can grasp the concept of reaching out and touching, what could change for you? What could be transformed? What could be made whole?

Throughout the Bible, the interactions with Christ detail a God who cares, one who is concerned about what might be troubling you, what you might need to let go of, and what you might need to grab hold of.

Be it unto you according to your faith, according to your response. Jesus is Lord. What is your response? Jesus is here. What is your response? Jesus is coming again. What is your response?

# Who Are You And What Are You Doing In My Shoes

The living Word of God provides us with revelation, inspiration, and illumination. In essence, the Spirit of God, through His presence, brings to life a dead letter that otherwise goes unknown, unnoticed, or only read. The combination of the written word and the Holy Ghost enables understanding and encouragement through the lens of God's light.

A deeper grasp of what is available is highlighted in an often-quoted scripture that says: "But as it is written, Eye hath not seen, nor ear heard, neither have entered into the heart of man, the things which God hath prepared for them that love him."

At first glance, it sounds as if this accolade of the future is just a wonderful preview of God's impending reward. Read on! Believe deeper!

The Spirit of God breathes life into this overarching preview. Newness and actuality spring forth with the very next verse. By His Spirit, God opens the eyes of our hearts. "But God hath revealed them unto us by his Spirit: for the Spirit searcheth all things, yea, the deep things of God." 1 Cor. 2:9-10.

Things not seen or understood in Isaiah's day are now unpacked by Christ to the Spirit-filled believers. The revelation of Jesus Christ for you who love Him is brought from a text into the hearts and minds of people who heretofore did not know the depths that exist in Him.

Are you scratching the surface or digging in with diligence? Whatever your answer is, it's not God's fault. God's intentions are clear; it is our execution that falters. Are you who God created you to be, or is another standing in your shoes?

God has given us everything we need to succeed in victorious Christian living. However, so often, believers allow giants to curse their God in public. They allow the powers that be to stand where they should stand. Prayers and praises become conditional. Morality is seen as subjective or offensive. We cede our God-given potential to another.

Years ago, as part of a leadership team for men's ministry, we settled on "Men of Valor" for a name. The phrase comes from Gideon's life calling and experience in Judges. Through this scripture, God relays to us that His ways for us are higher than our own without Him. God calls Gideon a mighty Man of Valor before Gideon ever arrives at that understanding of himself. You do the same.

Situations can sideline us from the action while our enemies enjoy the territory that belongs to us. God's design for Gideon lay just over the hill. While Gideon was hiding from his calling, his enemy stood where he belonged.

This truth unfolds in Judges, Chapter 6. Gideon's purposed existence had become marred by his hiding out to merely survive when he was meant to thrive. His enemy was camped in the position of his victory. While Gideon labored in Ophrah, his opponents enjoyed their spoils in Jezreel.

A deep dive into these positions reveals that while Gideon hid in his passive position, the Midianites occupied ground that represented God's design for his people.

The word Ophrah is rooted in a meaning of immaturity, the feminine tense of a baby deer. The word Jezreel is rooted in masculine definitions of "God sows" and "mighty men like him."

In the physical, the Midianites had stolen Israel's harvest. In the spiritual, the enemy possessed the ground of your calling and position in Christ. Fast forward to now. Who is standing in the position of your victory?

Does fear curse the calm that is found in Christ? Does drunkenness fill the shoes of your sobriety? Do excuses eliminate your efforts? Does immorality camp in the valley of your holiness? It may be time for an eviction.

You may need to hear the voice of the LORD calling you to fight. You may need to earnestly contend for the faith. God is calling mighty men and women to victory. Will you go? Will you stand? Will you fill those shoes?

# Longing For Home

With every passing day, it seems that the thought of heaven grows a little bit sweeter. I'm sure that life has a natural way of making the body tire as that outward man perishes. Perhaps another aspect of that growing desire is missing those that have already gone on ahead of us.

I do believe, though, that there is an even more essential part of longing for our heavenly home. That is, as we get to know Jesus better, we also realize that the best is yet to come.

When the lamb becomes the lion, the crucified is realized as the glorified, and we, as believers, will share in that glory. It excites me to think about the fact that the King of all kingdoms has included us in His inheritance. That is a promise.

To feel closer than ever before to what Jesus is preparing for us is exhilarating. Let your faith in Christ grow. Let your focus be above, and your feet be upon the ground. How beautiful is that vision? Just think, we should want as many as the Lord our God shall call to share in the promise of eternity. May your walk be one that leads all others home.

# Make Something Happen

I remember years ago reading a children's story about being aware. It was entitled something along the lines of, "Nothing ever happens on my block." It's about a young one who is looking for excitement, but exciting things seem to only happen in other places. The moral of the story was that exciting things were happening all around him, but the child was unaware because of despair.

Like despair, discouragement and disappointment have a way of paralyzing an individual from moving forward. Today we are called to serve a virtual world that is different than any ever world we have ever served before.

Many young people spend countless hours following and liking the stories of others. They think that the proverbial grass is always greener on the other side. Sometimes we do the same as saints of God. Whether it's a church or just a group of believers that we are a part of, we often opt for talk more than the walk. We look at others enjoying success and fall into a type of envy that is debilitating. We start everything with the "Well, if…" way of looking at things. Well, if we had more people, money, time, etc. We paint a picture that is virtual while reality sits in the corner waiting for us.

I want to encourage you not to base your success or failure on anyone else with no excuses and no "well ifs." Just be the you that God created you to be. Be busy doing what you can and do it well. Soon the righteous principle of victory for the faithful will kick in.

# Constant In Change

In every aspect of life, change happens. Often it throws us off our game. It throws a wrench into our thoughts and plans.

Someone once said that if you wanted to see God laugh, tell him of your plans. Our plans can include things that never materialize. God's plan does not. In fact, nothing surprises him. He knew what every day of your life would be like. Many people live struggling against God's will when surrender is the viable option. Not a surrender to the circumstances or struggles but rather to remain faithful throughout the journey.

Whether you are building a barn or thinking of what to wear, you seem to always remain constant in the fray. People need the anchors in life that a surrendered soul can provide. God does not change. Our center and foundation in life should be Christ and him crucified. When that is actualized, others will benefit from your walk, so walk worthy.

# Until The Next Time

Life is full of seasons of fellowship, labor, and rest. I've often longed for a fellowship that would be closer and last longer. Being a small part of a large body of believers, there is often a great physical distance in some of these fellowships that we enjoy with family members of the faith. In those specific relationships, there is a special bond that is enjoyed even though you may be miles apart. It's based on trust. It's a trust that our brotherhood and sisterhood remain when all else might fail. It's an open invitation.

Sadly though, and without fail, the news of an individual who has failed in their Christian walk makes its way to the surface. I often think that maybe if we were closer, that might not have happened. However, I'm not so sure about that.

The reason for this thought is that a person's walking away has more to do with what is inside them than what is outside. I long for unbreakable bonds of brotherhood. One that stands the test of time and distance. In the scripture, the verse that says the Lord watch between us while we are apart comes to mind. It is my prayer that the body of believers everywhere will hold true until we all dwell together in our Heavenly home.

# Get In The Game

I know that this will not apply to all. Many of us are engaged day in and day out in ministry, and we are thankful for each one that is laboring in the field and giving of themselves

This call is to the sidelines. Spiritual warfare requires an all-hands-on-deck. This call reminds me of a time when a naval vessel might encounter the enemy. The call would sound, "Man, your battle stations!" I believe that alarm is to some of our saints on the sidelines. Throughout life, I have experienced seasons where I was watching as others did spiritual warfare without my help. The Lord reminded me of a scripture that asked, "Shall your brother go to war, and you sit here?"

At times, I have allowed myself to become distracted. There are other problems that cause good people to simply watch while others do. Disappointment, discouragement, family issues, lack of funds, and personal spiritual issues can and will sideline Christians on a daily basis. I'm calling for you to get in the game. Put your hand on the plow.

Don't doubt and certainly don't delay. The time is now. If life has sidelined you for action, hear me now. Get in the day. Today is your day. The Lord is speaking and calling up those who have enlisted. Now is the time. Your brothers and sisters need you. Be strong in the Lord and in the power of his might.

# Sell Some Shoes

I heard a story recently that reminded me how much attitudes towards situations can make a difference.

The story goes something like this. A young man was hired to sell shoes. He was tasked with going to another country and representing his product. Upon arrival and to his dismay, he realized the people of that nation did not even wear shoes. He was so disappointed that he, in his defeat, called the Home Office and requested a ticket for a flight home. So, he returned along with his shipment of unsold shoes.

A second man was hired to go to the same country. He arrived with the shipment of the same shoes. When he stepped from the plane and saw that they had no shoes, he immediately made his way to a phone to call back to the Home Office and requested yet another shipment of shoes. In his excitement, he went on and on about being in a great market where all the people needed shoes.

Wherever you find yourself today, thrive in that place. Grow in that place. Live in that moment. May the zeal of the Lord accomplish his desire for his kingdom, and may he do it through you.

# Focus

The Lord has spoken into my heart and had me minister along the lines of focus.

Life has a way of knocking you down from time to time. Situations beyond our control often distract believers from the tasks that are at hand. The best advice that I have found is to focus on what is most important.

That would have us looking up instead of down. In this life, there are many temporary things. There is only one eternal one. The opportunity to follow Christ is the element of life that deserves our devoted focus.

The time we waste on circumstance is lost. To set our affections on things above is the key to successful Christian Living.

If you want to live in victory, you must look past now. Look past life's disappointments. Look past all the failures of others as well as those of your own making. Look to Jesus, the author, and finisher of your faith. If anyone ever has, you can. In doing so, the eternal will impact your life here in a way that can make a difference for others. That is what faith is all about.

# The Seasoning of Hope

Life has a way of bringing to bare pressures that sometimes seem too much to endure. Situations that we all face will if allowed to, rule the day. Most of these come in some unmanageable fashion, for instance, others.

People have a way of presenting issues that we, in and of ourselves, can not change. They leave us feeling powerless against the circumstances. No amount of talk can exact the needed change. The emotional strain can be unbearable.

Learning to hope for the best and deal with the rest is an art form. It is, in essence, trusting God in an ultimate act of faith. The world mimics this truth in the phrase *casara sara* or whatever will be, will be.

A Christian's hope is to transcend a simple relegation to the acceptance of negative circumstances in the hopes of a better eternal outcome. If only this world and its trappings garner our hope, we will live in disappointment. Our overarching hope must be in the eternal.

In this world, we desire justice. However, someone can receive justice in this world while a judgment awaits in another. We must focus on trust in God and allow Him to empower us to face this world's injustices.

In this life, we desire others to bear the fruit of salvation. We often despair when we do not see those signs that accompany faith in God. Sprinkling hope in every situation gives us the spark needed to endure all things.

I can not imagine the devastation that Christ's crucifixion had on his followers. Scattered is one way it's described. Of course, confusion, disappointment, and discouragement thought that they had won those hearts and minds.

However, the resurrection power of the Spirit of God brought the good news that revealed victory through tribulation. Yesterday's disappointment is now today's encouragement, and that is not only for today and tomorrow but forever.

That forever focus gives us the hope to make it through all things for the glory that awaits the believer. We needlessly struggle against trials and tribulations when, in fact, the hope in the joy of the Lord can strengthen us beyond comprehension.

Through the fire, there is hope. Through the flood, there is hope. Through death and life, there is hope. Season your reason with the flavor of hope in Christ.

We must hope for Christian maturity. We must hope for the lost. We must hope for a better tomorrow. In those hopes, our outlook and our attitudes can change.

In that change, peace of mind replaces pessimism. Joy overtakes despair. Love wins. God's promises become our focal point. That help and hope take center stage.

Let your life be the flavor of hope!

# Yesterday, Today, And Tomorrow

There are some things that will be exactly the same every day. There are some things that change even minute by minute. One generation passes away, and another takes its place. Trees blossom, and the leaves fall. Beauty fades, and new babies are introduced.

Yesterday, we celebrated all those things that change in light of the things that do not. As we enjoyed a Sunday lunch for pastors' appreciation, I thought of the youth that had conducted the service. What an awesome experience!

My wife and I appreciate the many encouraging aspects of pastor appreciation month. To be honest, it is somewhat awkward to be a focal point in that regard. This morning though, we feel blessed to have enjoyed all of our yesterday's showing up in the next generation of ministry.

Yesterday we planted. Yesterday we watered. Today we celebrate God's increases. My mind went back to the many children's churches, Sunday school classes, and youth group sessions that have culminated in ministry for today and tomorrow. The fruit of eternity was on display.

As I reflect on all of the baby dedications and baptisms, my heart melts that those individuals now stand in Christ and behind the microphone. The display of fruit that remains is encouraging to pastors.

The local church is the crux of the ministry of eternity. It's where Jesus is taught, received, and realized generation after generation. It's where the believing is both called and sent. It's all of our yesterday's realized today impacting tomorrow.

No second-guessing Monday morning quarterbacking is going on today. Today, we are proud of what the Lord is doing at Crossroads Chapel Church of God of Prophecy in Palm Harbor.

Jesus is the same yesterday, today, and forever. Seasons come, and seasons go. People come, and people go. Situations and circumstances come and go, but Jesus never fails.

# Living the Dream

I have a few friends who, when asked how they are doing, they respond, "Living the dream." Others might say, "Blessed and highly favored. " I repeat what a good friend of mine always says and mostly just answer, "Excellent!"

I feel fortunate not because of fortune. I'm thankful for my life experience, which has included many highs and lows. I appreciate every day as an opportunity to make a difference for Christ.

My reflections and memories today are filled with a fondness for friends and family who have graduated to their heavenly reward. That is the dream or goal of every believer.

One of my dreams was to own and restore a Harley that was my age. My friend Zman got a hold of an older project bike that I was a little jealous of. I would stop by and admire its craftsmanship, all the time encouraging him to get it going. We often have too many irons in the fire to live out all of our dreams.

One night recently, I had a dream that I was riding that bike. As fate would have it, my friend Zman went home to be with the Lord. Many of his earthly dreams were unfinished, but his earthly work for the Lord was done. It reminds me a little of Christ's words, "It is finished," but the dream lives on.

As a minister, Zman had a dream and a vision. He was inspired by a man who also had a vision of Christ's work for him in this present world. Barry Mason was that inspiration. A man saved by the grace of God, through the fortitude of a praying mother, was literally snatched from hell by the Holy Spirit.

Barry's ministry and work was unique, to say the least. A ministry to the biker community captured the heart and minds of both of these men. Zman and Barry had a dream that would be known as Heaven's Saints. They were living their dream.

Through all of life's ups and downs, they kept the dream alive. I, too, was inspired and encouraged by them and cherished their friendship and brotherhood. Now their mission lives on through us who remain. We are living the dream.

Today when the Heaven's Saints get together, we often ask anyone who personally knew Barry before he graduated over 15 years ago to stand. Those numbers are diminished seemingly by the day, yet the vision of the Saints is stronger now than ever before. We are ministering and realizing his dream and vision.

With the help of my good friend Mickey, one of my dreams is coming true. Through some horse trading with Z's family, I ended up with the one-day project bike from his garage. I found out it was a 66. I was born at 65. So, in essence, we were in the factory at the same time.

Acts say that God's promise is to as many as the Lord our God shall call. One generation passes away, another takes the helm, and we ride on. Barry, his bride Fran and Zmans ministry live on through their families and the family of the Heaven's Saints Motorcycle Ministry.

Two thoughts. Encourage someone today who you admire in the faith. We should not wait for memories and reflection for the honor. Secondly, take up your cross and live out the ministry of your generation, even with all of its highs and lows. Christ's vision for his bride must be lived out through you, here and now.

Ride on!

Made in the USA
Columbia, SC
20 February 2023

12638381R00070